James, Earl of Moray: Regent of Scotland

A Tudor Times Insight

By Tudor Times

Published by Tudor Times Ltd

Tudor Times Insights

Tudor Times Insights are books collating articles from our website www.tudortimes.co.uk which is a repository for a wide variety of information about the Tudor and Stewart period 1485 – 1625. There you can find material on People, Places, Daily Life, Military & Warfare, Politics & Economics and Religion. The site has a Book Review section, with author interviews and a book club. It also features comprehensive family trees, and a 'What's On' event list with information about forthcoming activities relevant to the Tudors and Stewarts.

Titles in the Series

Profiles

Katherine Parr: Henry VIII's Sixth Queen
James IV: King of Scots
Lady Margaret Pole: Countess of Salisbury
Thomas Wolsey: Henry VIII's Cardinal
Marie of Guise: Regent of Scotland
Thomas Cromwell: Henry VIII's Chief Minister
Lady Penelope Devereux: Sir Philip Sidney's Muse
James V: Scotland's Renaissance King
Lady Katherine Grey: Tudor Prisoner
Sir William Cecil: Elizabeth I's Chief Minister
Lady Margaret Douglas: Countess of Lennox
Sir James Melville: Scottish Ambassador
Tudors & Stewarts 2015: A collection of 12 Profiles
Lady Margaret Beaufort
Mary I: Queen of England

People

Who's Who in Wolf Hall

Politics & Economy

Field of Cloth of Gold
Succession: The Tudor Problem
The Pilgrimage of Grace and Exeter Conspiracy

Contents

Preface 7

Family Tree 8

Chapter 1: Early Life...9

Chapter 2: Youth 11

Chapter 3: The French Marriage...14

Chapter 4: The Lords of the Congregation 16

Chapter 5: Rebellion..19

Chapter 6: The Wars of the Congregation 22

Chapter 7: Protestant Reformation 24

Chapter 8: Negotiations with Queen Mary.............................27

Chapter 9: The Return of the Queen 30

Chapter 10: A Wife and Two Earldoms 33

Chapter 11: The Overthrow of Huntly.....................................36

Chapter 12: The Queen's Marriage 39

Chapter 13: The Chaseabout Raid...41

Chapter 14: Assassination..44

Chapter 15: Planning a Murder...47

Chapter 16: Accusations...50

Chapter 17: Mary's Escape 53

Chapter 18: York Commission 56

Part 2: Aspects of Moray's Life..61

Chapter 19: Following the Footsteps of James, Earl of Moray........61

Chapter 20: Three Book Reviews 68

Bibliography 75

Preface

Lord James Stewart, half-brother of Mary, Queen of Scots, was the son of a King, but as he was illegitimate, could never be King himself. Resigned to seeing his father's Crown pass to his baby half-sister, he was a loyal and supportive stepson to the Regent until religion came between them. When his sister returned to Scotland he became her closest adviser, but their relationship deteriorated when Mary did not always accept his advice, resulting in murder and civil war.

Whilst Moray spent the majority of his life in lowland Scotland he also travelled to the north-east of the country and made at least two journeys to France and several to England, sometimes on diplomatic missions, but also as an exile.

To some, he was 'the Good Regent', but to others he was the betrayer of his sister, and even a secret accessory to murder...

This book contains James, Earl of Moray's Life Story and additional articles.

The material was first published on www.tudortimes.co.uk

Family Tree

Lord James STEWART
1st Earl of Moray

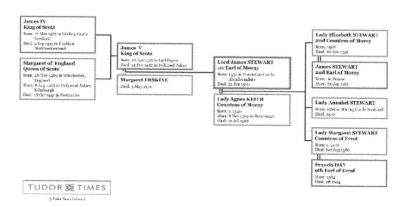

Chapter 1: Early Life

King James V of Scotland was notorious for the number of mistresses he had. One of the women to whom he seems to have been most closely attached was Margaret Erskine. Margaret was the daughter of John, 5th Lord Erskine, an important member of James V's court and a close adviser of the King's, who was so well regarded by the King that, in 1535 he had been sent by James to fetch the insignia of the Order of the Garter, bestowed on the King by his uncle, Henry VIII.

The fact that Margaret was the King's mistress did not seem to trouble her father in the slightest. It was common for Scottish Kings to have mistresses amongst the ranks of the nobility, and no-one seems to have thought the worse of the ladies. In this case, Margaret had more than just her father to consider. In 1524, or possibly 1527, long before she became involved with James, she had married Sir Robert Douglas of Lochleven, by whom she had several children.

The presence of a husband was no more of an impediment than that of a father and in around 1531 Margaret bore King James a son. In common with the practice of Scottish Kings, who had no reservations about acknowledging their illegitimate children, the boy was known as Lord James Stewart. King James already had an older illegitimate son by Elizabeth Shaw also called James Stewart, and would have more children by different mothers.

Despite his other amours, King James seems to have genuinely loved Margaret – so much so that in 1536, he considered marrying her. The Treaty of Rouen signed with France in 1519 when James was a mere seven years old, had provided for him to marry a French princess, but by 1536 King François of France was showing signs of reneging on the deal. He was reluctant to allow his daughter Madeleine, who was of uncertain health, to travel to damp Scotland. James, taking umbrage at this lack of respect for his position, decided that a marriage to a woman who had already borne him a son might be the answer.

Had Margaret been unmarried at the time, all might have been well but Sir Robert Douglas was still alive. King James arranged an annulment of the Douglas marriage by the Scottish bishops which was easily granted, but he still needed a Papal dispensation to marry Margaret. Unfortunately, the Pope would not grant the necessary consent. King James, perhaps taking note of the turmoil into which Henry VIII's life and realm had been thrown by an attempt to marry without papal blessing, decided to accept Pope Paul III's ruling and put aside any thought of marrying Margaret Erskine, although it was rumoured in July 1536, that they had married, and the lady later maintained that she was, indeed, his wife.

Since she did not say anything until after the King's death, and he proceeded to marry twice, it does not seem likely that there was any valid marriage between them.

Having given up the idea of marrying Margaret and legitimising Lord James, the King was still mindful of his obligations towards the boy. On 31 August 1536, he was granted lands, including the castle at Tantallon—confiscated from the Earl of Angus, the King's hated step-father. Two years later, Lord James was named Prior of St Andrews, despite being only seven years old. This practice of the Scottish Kings of giving high Church offices to their illegitimate offspring was one of the most blatant elements of corruption in the Scottish Church prior to the Reformation.

Lord James seems to have been brought up largely at his father's court. The King's marriages, first, to Madeleine of France, and second, to Marie of Guise, in no way interfered with the King showing his affection for his son. Lord James seems to have shared a household with his illegitimate half-sister, Lady Jean Stewart, daughter of Elizabeth Beaton; the other Lord James Stewart, now Abbot of Kelso; Lord Robert Stewart; Lord Alexander Stewart; and Lord John Stewart (the prevalence of illegitimate scions of the royal house explains the extraordinary plethora of families named Stewart in 15th and 16th century Scotland, who are hard to disentangle).

There are records in King James' accounts for Lord James' maintenance – including expensive fabric for clothes. Black velvet, grey satin from Venice, and fine linen were all delivered to the King's own master tailor for clothes, hats, shoes and hose. As a son of the King he was permitted to wear purple velvet and have fur trimmed clothes. As two of the King's illegitimate sons were called James it can be difficult to be certain who was receiving what but there can be no doubt that King James treated all his off-spring generously. Three servants are mentioned serving Lord James – Walter Bell, Donald Beg and Janet Ferguson, who was Lord James' laundress, and a cook, Thomas Dury.

As only one of so many illegitimate children, and not the eldest, Lord James cannot have had any idea when he was a child of being named his father's heir, especially when Queen Marie of Guise had two sons in quick succession. Although both boys died as infants in April 1541, the Queen was soon pregnant again, giving birth to a daughter, Mary, on 8 December 1542.

Chapter 2: Youth

A week after the birth of Mary, disaster struck Scotland when James V died at the age of 30. Lord James was around 11 years old, and, together with all his siblings, faced years of uncertainty as the weak Regent, the

Earl of Arran, tried, first, to work with the English, then, as their demands became too great, reverted to the traditional alliance with France, whilst the Dowager Queen Marie, and Cardinal Beaton also tussled for control of the country.

During these years, the Protestant Reformation began to gain a toe-hold in Scotland. It advanced particularly swiftly in Fife, the area in which the primary bishopric, that of St Andrew's, was based, and where, in theory, Lord James himself was Prior of the Abbey. It was at St Andrew's that the first great Scottish Reformer, George Wishart, was burnt in 1546, but not before spreading his message to other converts, including John Knox, who was to play an important part in Lord James' life.

That Lord James remained within Court circles after his father's death seems to be confirmed by the fact that, in 1548, when the young Queen Mary was sent to France for her upbringing, under the protection of Lord Erskine, James's grandfather, James himself accompanied her. He was by now around 18 years old and, after Mary joined the court, he went to study at the University of Paris, although he does not seem to have stayed long in France.

In 1551 Lord James visited France again as part of the entourage who accompanied the Queen Dowager, Marie of Guise on her visit to her daughter. He would therefore have passed through England on the return journey and it was probably then that he first made the acquaintance of the John Knox, who, following a punishment stint in French galleys, was chaplain to Edward VI. This may have been the point when Lord James himself began to take an interest in the Reformed faith.

Scotland was still unsettled – although the English had given up the idea of conquering the country by force, there were growing factions within the Scottish nobility who saw an alliance with an England becoming increasingly Protestant under Edward VI, as preferable to domination by Catholic France. Nevertheless, it would not be true to say at this point that the divisions were on religious grounds – there were Protestants who favoured a French-inclined policy, and Catholics who disliked it.

In May 1553, it was reported in a letter by the Imperial Ambassador, Jehan Sheyfve, that, in an effort to get rid of the Regent, the Duke of Chatelherault (despite the French title, this was James Hamilton, Earl of Arran), Marie of Guise was proposing Lord James as Regent for his half-sister. Although the letter is usually assumed to refer to Lord James, as noted before, he had an older half-brother of the same name, and Scheyve may have been referring to him, given that Lord James was only twenty-two. He did, however, have a close relationship with Marie of Guise, and when she was finally appointed as Regent he worked closely with her.

South of the border, the Calvinist-inspired government of Edward VI had been replaced by the Catholic regime of his sister, Mary I. The control of Scotland and England by two Catholic women did not in any way lead to a political rapprochement between the countries. Mary of England was innately suspicious of any pro-French Scottish government, and, once married to the King of Spain, was supportive of the Spanish-Imperial side in the interminable Franco-Spanish conflict, whilst Marie, was, naturally, supportive of the Scottish-French alliance cemented by the marriage of her daughter Mary, Queen of Scots to the French Dauphin.

Marie of Guise also differed, initially, from her English counterpart in having a less hard-line attitude towards religious conformity. The Catholic counterrevolution in England led to a number of Protestant preachers taking exile in Scotland and their following was growing.

Marie of Guise was by nature inclined to tolerance and whether from a genuine dislike of persecution or for political expediency, no attempts were initially made to combat the growth of Protestantism. In fact many even believed that she herself might convert.

One of these returning exiles was none other than John Knox. He arrived in Edinburgh in September 1555 and met a number of leading Protestants, including John Erskine of Dun, and William Maitland of Lethington, who was Secretary to Marie of Guise. Maitland was a strong supporter of alliance between England and Scotland and opposed to French dominance. Another convert was James' uncle, John, 6th Lord Erskine. James himself had not yet firmly joined the Protestant group, he was still attending Mass with his stepmother. Nevertheless he was sufficiently impressed with Knox to add his voice to the other Lords who were encouraging Knox to preach publicly in Edinburgh. Edinburgh was still too Catholic for such a scheme to be possible but at Easter 1556, Knox preached publicly for the first time in Scotland at Calder.

Chapter 3: The French Marriage

Shortly afterwards, Knox wrote to Marie of Guise exhorting her to abandon her faith and bring Scotland into the kingdom of the elect. Although he tried to word his admonition tactfully, his zeal and uncompromising belief in his own righteousness led him to take a moralising tone with the Regent that she found ludicrous. She might be willing to permit a degree of tolerance but she was not going to take advice from a lowly preacher. Knox, dismayed that he had not persuaded the Regent to convert, retired to Geneva in high dudgeon. He displayed his disappointment in his *First Blast of the Trumpet against the*

Monstrous Regiment of Women, in which he set out his unshakeable belief that rule by a woman was counter to the Word of God.

This was certainly not a belief confined to Knox, but, for most people, stable, legitimate government, even if led by a woman, was a higher priority than the abstract concept of male dominance and James, although he probably would have preferred a legal system that rejected feminine rule, left no evidence that he ever objected to his sister's position as Queen on the grounds of her gender.

In 1557, James, increasingly reformist in outlook, together with the committed Protestants, his uncle Lord Erskine, Lord Glencairn and Lord Lorne, invited Knox to return to Scotland. He took some persuading but eventually agreed to come. When he was already on his way James and the others changed their minds and told him not to return – the political situation was complex and sensitive, and they knew that Knox would always put honesty before expediency. Knox, grievously offended by this dithering, sent a letter to the Lords exhorting them to do their duty and make every attempt to bring Scotland out of the darkness and into the light.

James and the others ignored this missive – they were too concerned about the political situation. The time had come for the young Queen Mary to be married to François, the Dauphin of France. Lord James was one of the Scottish Commissioners sent to negotiate the terms and conditions of the marriage in December 1557 and attend the ceremony. On the surface, all seemed well, as the marriage treaty confirmed that all of the rights and privileges of the Scottish government would remain the same and provided that, if Queen Mary failed to bear a son and had only daughters, the Crown of Scotland would pass to her eldest daughter in accordance with Scottish, rather than French law, which did not recognise women's right to succeed to the Crown. Of course, if Queen

Mary were to have a son he would inherit both France and Scotland. There was distinct unease in Scotland about much of this – had they escaped a forced union by marriage with England only to be faced with a slightly-less forced union with France?

Lord James and the other Scottish Lords would presumably have been even more nervous had they known that Queen Mary had been inveigled into signing a secret document leaving her throne, in the case of childlessness, to the French Crown rather than to her actual heir – the Duke of Chatelherault. The Duke's place in the succession had been confirmed as part of the agreement he made to step down from the Regency in favour of Marie de Guise. As it happened, the Earl of Lennox contested the Duke's claims, and this would lead to later troubles. There was never any discussion about the possibility of Lord James being named as an alternative. The other Lord James Stewart had died in 1557, so James was now the eldest surviving of James V's illegitimate sons.

Chapter 4: The Lords of the Congregation

As more of the Lords converted to the new faith, Marie of Guise tried to follow a path of toleration, permitting both Protestant and Catholic services to continue side-by-side – her ultimate goal was not religious uniformity, but to keep her daughter Mary recognised as Queen, and in control of the country. Unfortunately religious tolerance was not acceptable in 16th century Europe either to Catholics or to Protestants and both sides wanted more – the Catholics to follow the crack-downs on 'heresy' being implemented in France, Spain and England, and the Protestants to overthrow the ancient religion, obedience to the Pope, and the alliance with France.

In 1558 the Protestant Lords in Scotland formed themselves into a group called the Lords of the Congregation. Lord James did not immediately join this group. He seems to have been attached to his stepmother, Queen Marie, and reluctant to enter into open rebellion.

So long as Mary I of England lived, the Lords of the Congregation had no external power to support them against the strength of France, but the situation changed with her death in November 1558. The new Queen, Elizabeth I, was known to be sympathetic to the Protestant cause (although she advanced slowly at home), and more importantly for the Protestant lords, her chief minister, William Cecil, was well-known personally to both James and Maitland of Lethington (a leading Protestant, despite being Queen Marie's Secretary) and was a committed Protestant.

In November 1558, although not a fully-fledged member of the Congregation, James was one of the signatories to a letter to John Knox, again inviting him to return to Scotland. Knox, at first hesitating after the debacle of his wasted trip in 1557, eventually arrived Scotland on 10 May 1559. Two days later he rode to Dundee to meet the Protestant leaders, although James remained with the Regent Queen Marie.

Queen Marie, now that her immediate object of having Queen Mary married to the Dauphin of France had been achieved, and perhaps alarmed by the spread of the new faith, changed her previous policy of toleration and moved against the Protestant preachers, planning to have them outlawed and exiled. On being urged to keep her promise of toleration she informed her horrified Councillors that rulers should not be coerced into keeping promises that were no longer convenient. The banned preachers assembled at Perth. Worried lest they be seen to be an army, rather than a peaceful gathering of preachers, Erskine of Dun sent a message to the Regent assuring her that their aims were peaceful. The

Regent listened to him and agreed that the summons to Stirling that she had previously issued to the preachers should be abandoned. Foolishly, in hindsight, she again went back on her word and the preachers were outlawed.

Knox began to preach in Perth. He was a man of extraordinary rhetorical power, and, following one of his sermons, an iconoclastic riot broke out, which completely destroyed the interior of the Church of St John's as well as those of the Friary and the Charterhouse in the town. Knox, whilst not entirely condoning these acts, referring to them as carried out by the *'rascal multitude'*, did not heartily condemn them either.

The Regent could not accept such a challenge to her rule and, raising troops, marched on Perth. She was still accompanied by Lord James, whom she sent, together with the Earl of Argyll and Lord Sempill, to ask the Protestant leaders why they were holding Perth against their lawful ruler.

Lord James visited Knox in his lodgings and received messages that the Protestants were not rebelling, but defending true religion. As was usual with Knox he gilded the lily by informing Marie that her religion was *'a superstition devised by the brain of man'* and that he was a better friend to her people than she. Unsurprisingly, the Regent was *'somewhat offended'* by Knox's message. Nevertheless she continued to negotiate and it was agreed that both armies would disband and the Queen Regent be free to enter the city. No punishment was to be carried out and no French troops would be left in the city. Parliament was to be called to resolve the differences between the groups. No French garrison was left, however 400 Scottish troops loyal to the Crown were stationed in the city. This was declared to be a breach of the agreement by the Regent on the basis that pay for the Scottish troops came from France.

There was now complete breakdown between the Congregation and Queen Marie. She continued to state that the Lord of the Congregation were not necessarily motivated by religion but wished to overthrow her lawful authority. She summoned more troops from France. The Lords of the Congregation requested help from England, which Elizabeth was reluctant to openly grant, despite the persuasions of Sir William Cecil.

The appearance of French troops on Scottish soil led many of the nobles to believe that the French were as bad as the English, whilst the common people do not seem to have been markedly in favour of supporting either side.

Lord James, having put off the evil moment as long as possible, was now forced to choose sides. On 11th June 1559 he, together with the Earl of Argyll, joined the Lords of the Congregation and requested help from Protestant England.

Chapter 5: Rebellion

All-out civil war seemed likely. Queen Marie was seriously ill, but a new army was raised under the Duke of Chatelherault and her French Councillor, d'Oysel. The opposing armies marched into Fife but Lord Lindsay was able to negotiate an agreement whereby the French troops would withdraw, the Queen Regent would be able to enter Fife, should she choose to, but the Protestants would be granted freedom of religion. In return, the Lords of the Congregation would disband their army.

The mob which had rioted in Perth was now advancing on Scone Abbey. This ancient Abbey was an important symbol of the Scottish Crown and the Lords of the Congregation had no more desire to see it damaged that had Queen Marie. Knox also disapproved of rioting and rebellion. He joined with Lord James and the Earl of Argyll to try to prevent the destruction but even his word was not sufficient to prevent the sacking of the Abbey and the Palace nearby.

Lord James, Argyll and Knox left Perth with their army and captured Stirling. This was a significant gain for the Lords, as Stirling's location made it key to the holding of Scotland. In the early morning of 30th June 1559 the army of the Lords of the Congregation marched into Edinburgh. Almost overnight, the city was denuded of the outward symbols of the Catholic faith. The Regent issued orders to the Congregation to leave Edinburgh within six hours but her orders were ignored.

Marie sent for troops from France and the Lords retaliated by again requesting help from England. Elizabeth I, who disliked Knox almost as much as Queen Marie did, refused to be seen to openly aid rebellious subjects. There was also some doubt in English minds as to whether the Lords of the Congregation were really defending religion or were merely hoping to benefit themselves. Nevertheless William Cecil worked on Elizabeth to support the Lords in secret.

Once the Protestants had captured the Royal Mint, Marie decided to march on Edinburgh although she did not have sufficient troops. She captured Leith but neither side was anxious for outright war. Another agreement was reached whereby the people of Edinburgh could choose their form of worship - the Protestants could worship in St Giles Kirk, where Knox had been set up as Minister, and the Roman Catholics could hear mass at Holyrood. The Congregation would return the coining irons for the royal mint, which they had taken, hand over Holyrood Palace, which they had captured, and withdraw from the city. They would continue in their allegiance to Queen Mary (still in France) and the Regent.

Whether this would have been a long-term solution is doubtful – Marie had shown that her word could not always be trusted, and it is hard to imagine that Knox would have tolerated the continuance of Catholicism. But before the agreement could be tested, a cataclysmic event in France changed the scene entirely. Henri II, who had been a strong support of Marie, was killed in a jousting accident. The new King of France, the husband of Mary, Queen of Scots, was young and in poor health. It was also obvious that the new King and Queen would be dominated by Mary's trenchantly Catholic uncles, the Duke of Guise and the Cardinal of Lorraine, who were the brothers of the Regent.

For both England, and the Scots who were uncomfortable with French power, this turn of events seemed to presage an even stronger domination of Scotland by France. This fear, together with a hint that Elizabeth I might marry his son, the Earl of Arran, was one of the levers used to persuade the Duke of Chatelherault to abandon the Regent. Arran, who had been held as a hostage in France until smuggled out by the English ambassador, had converted to Protestantism and with his return to Scotland he was able to persuade his father to join the Lords of the Congregation.

The Lords, including Lord James, entered Edinburgh in force and suspended Marie's position as Queen Regent. Allegiance to Queen Mary and King François was confirmed, but the role of the Regency would be taken by a Council of 30 including Lord James. This did not resolve the situation, as French troops were approaching and it was by no means certain that the Lords of Congregation could resist them.

To a degree, the motives of the Lords were still suspect. Cecil wrote a memorandum for Queen Elizabeth, with a list of actions that England's emissary, Ralph Sadler, ought to undertake in Scotland, which included not just 'nourishing' the faction against the French, but also:

'To explore the very truth, whether Lord James enterprises towards the Crown for himself or no? And if he do, and the Duke [Chatelherault] be cold in his own cause, it may not be amisse to let Lord James follow his own device, without interference.' That is, that England should not interfere to prevent James from usurping his sister's Crown.

There is no evidence as to whether James had any immediate intentions in this direction, but he cannot have helped believing that it would be better for him to be King of Scots, than for vicarious rule from France, which looked set to continue indefinitely.

Chapter 6: The Wars of the Congregation

Whether or not he had any hidden motives, James and the other Lords of the Congregation were in constant touch with Cecil, assuring him that, if England were to give a show of support, those Scottish Lords who had not joined the Congregation, but who were showing no eagerness to support the Regent, would defect to the Congregation. They also informed him, in late December 1559, that Marie had invited the Earl of Lennox to return to Scotland. Lennox had been exiled in England since the early 1540s.

Married to James V's half-sister, Lady Margaret Douglas (who, in terms of strict primogeniture had the best claim to be the heir to the English throne after Mary, Queen of Scots), Lennox and the Hamilton family, of which Chatelherault was the head, were at daggers drawn. Lennox believed his claim to be Queen Mary's heir was stronger than Chatelherault's, and he had defected to the English side rather than support Chatelherault's Regency. By inviting him to return, Marie was making it clear that she no longer trusted the Hamiltons. Arran

(Chatelherault's son) and James asked Cecil to prevent Lennox leaving England.

Matters were coming to a head as the French troops Marie had requested began to arrive. The Lords feared that if the French took Stirling from them, they would be annihilated. They sent increasingly importunate letters to England, requesting support. The French were slightly hampered by Lord Erskine's threat to bombard Holyrood Palace (where Marie was) if they advanced. Lord James and Arran were at Dunfermline. Dunfermline is no distance at all now, with the bridge over the Firth of Forth, but in the 1550s, it would be several days march.

The French troops now assembled and took Leith – behaving as badly as conquering soldiers in foreign territories always do, and turning the population against the French alliance. Meanwhile, Elizabeth had at last consented to send support, and a number of English ships sailed up the Channel and into the Firth of Forth in January 1560. The French fleet had been badly damaged by winter storms and there were insufficient French troops to resist the English.

In February 1560 Elizabeth signed the Treaty of Berwick under which she took into her *protection* the realm of Scotland. This protection was to last for the entire duration of the marriage of Mary, Queen of Scots, to the King of France, and for one year thereafter. English troops would be sent to expel the French. In return the Scots would send troops to England should the French invade. As was customary, hostages were granted, including Lord James' half-brother, Sir Robert Douglas.

By March, even the Earl of Huntly, who remained firmly Catholic, was prepared to support the Lords of the Congregation (although there may have been an element of revenge in this, as Marie had curtailed his almost-king-like powers in the north of the country). Lord James announced this additional support in one of the regular letters he wrote to Elizabeth, keeping her informed of events. James was clearly not entirely convinced about Huntly's loyalty, as he asked Elizabeth and Cecil to keep Huntly's letters – 'thai wryttingis suld be kept in stoyr for all aventeures'.

There were now some 9,000 troops assembled in support of the Lords at Prestonpans. Marie, her health in terminal decline, retreated from Holyrood to the more easily defensible Edinburgh Castle, as the Congregation army, composed of English and Scots, besieged Leith, held by French and Scots.

Knowing her end was near, Marie made a final attempt to prevent civil war. She summoned a deputation, including James, from the Lords of the Congregation. The Lords complained about French influence and Marie replied that the presence of French troops had been approved by the Scottish Parliament and she would not send them away. Matters were at an impasse.

A few days later, Marie, on her deathbed, again sent for James and his colleagues. She forgave them all their offences against her and begged their forgiveness for any she had committed. She asked James and the Earl of Argyll to remain with her so James, presumably, was at his step-mother's side when she died early in the morning of 11 June 1560. Immediately following her death, the French troops withdrew and, with the death of Marie, it seemed that the Protestant faction would triumph.

Chapter 7: Protestant Reformation

The Lords of Congregation now entered into a second treaty with England - the Treaty of Edinburgh. Under this, a new Regency Council of

14 Lords was to be appointed, eight by Queen Mary and six by Parliament, although in practical terms the six would be chosen by the Lords. This was a level of democracy unknown in Europe. Elizabeth I would certainly have been horrified had it been suggested to *her* that Parliament should select her Council. Queen Mary refused to ratify this treaty, which also demanded the removal of all foreign troops from Scotland, despite the fact that the Lords of the Congregation continued to request English military aid.

Control in Scotland was now taken by re-taken by James Hamilton, Duke of Châtelherault, who had been a somewhat ineffectual Regent before Marie of Guise took office. He was supported by William Maitland of Lethington, and Lord James.

A Parliament, which became known as the Reformation Parliament, opened on 10 August 1560. The most important act passed was the Confession of Faith, together with legislation making it illegal to hear Catholic mass. The Reformed faith as set out in the Confession, was now the official religion of Scotland. The English Ambassador, Thomas Randolph, wrote to Cecil that he was surprised that the Confession had been passed – even though some of its stronger terms had been watered down on the advice of Maitland of Lethington. One of three Lords who voted against the Reformation Acts was John Stewart, Earl of Atholl.

Despite this fundamental disagreement, Atholl met with Lord James, and the Earl of Argyll, in September of 1560 to form a league against the Earl of Huntly, who was Atholl's rival for pre-eminence in the Highlands, and was, in fact, Atholl's father-in-law. (He was also Lord James' cousin, being, like him, a grandson of James IV). Argyll was later James' brother-in-law, married to Lady Jean Stewart. The three allies did not believe that Huntly would accept the new status quo, although at that time they had no evidence for their concerns.

As Huntly had not attended the Parliament, he was requested to confirm his approval of the business concluded there. He did so, but this does not seem to have been enough to allay the concerns of the others. They distrusted his having sent emissaries to France to Queen Mary.

In December 1560, another death occurred that would radically affect the position of James and the rest of the Regency Council in Scotland. King François, husband of their sovereign, Mary, Queen of Scots, died at the age of sixteen, leaving Mary a childless widow. Immediately, the Queen's mother-in-law, Catherine de Medici took the opportunity to oust the Guise family from power, and, as she disliked Mary intensely, it was soon apparent that there was no room for the eighteen year old girl in France.

Lord James was swiftly dispatched to France to advise his half-sister. The letter from Maitland of Lethington in which the Lords' plans were revealed to William Cecil, and hence to Elizabeth I, would surely have had him hanged as a traitor, had its contents come into Mary's hands. In it, he wrote that, should Queen Mary arrive with a naval force, her subjects could legitimately resist her, but that before they took such a step, they would consult with Elizabeth, by whose command they would be ruled. He presented the reasons why Lord James was to be sent to Mary:

'[Lord James] is zelous in religion and one off the precise Protestantes, knowen to be trew and constant, honest and not able to be corrupted; besides that nature must move her hyghnes to beare him some good will, and it is lyke that she will rather trust him then [than] any other.'

His task was to *'grope'* Mary's mind as to her intentions, but he would also, if granted a passport by Elizabeth, travel via England, both going and returning to France, so that he could share everything he learnt with the English government.

Maitland expressed at great length the problems faced by the Protestant Lords. By their actions, they had overthrown the government of the Queen's mother, entered into a treaty with the old enemy, England, and shown themselves as enemies of Queen Mary's religion – they were very nervous about what action she would take. Maitland, in particular, was talked of as *'a better Englishman'* even than the others – hardly likely to be appealing to Mary.

Chapter 8: Negotiations with Queen Mary

Lord James set out in February, accompanied by several lords, including the Laird of Pitarrow (John Wishart, probably a cousin of the martyr, George Wishart) who was described as *'a man mervileus wyse, discryte, and godly, with owte spotte or wryncle'*. Pitarrow seems to have been a close associate of Lord James and the two are often mentioned together.

Before Lord James arrived, Mary had received John Leslie, an emissary from the Earl of Huntly. He informed her that Huntly was prepared to support her with troops if she chose to land in his earldom, so that she could restore the Catholic faith – still the religion of the vast majority of ordinary Scots, and much of the nobility. He also warned her that Lord James had his eyes on her Crown.

Obviously, there was mutual distrust between James and Huntly - James may have been eyeing the Scottish Crown, or, even if he were not, Huntly may have genuinely believed Mary to be in danger from her brother – or he could have been trying to get the knife in first. Whilst events did not fall out exactly as Huntly anticipated, the eventual fate of the siblings suggests that James was not entirely uninterested in the Crown.

On 15 April 1561 Lord James arrived at San Dizier in north-eastern France. He spent five days with his half-sister and Mary was so impressed with him, perhaps remembering that despite all their differences he had stayed with her mother until Marie's death, she considered making him Regent during her continued absence. Unfortunately for him, however, she discovered that no sooner had he left her than he went straight Paris and talked to Sir Nicholas Throckmorton, the English ambassador there, following this up with a meeting with Queen Elizabeth and Sir William Cecil en route home. Nevertheless Mary was prepared to act on his advice. She would return to Scotland on the basis that no attempt would be made to overturn the Protestantism established by the Parliament of 1560. She would retain Lord James and Maitland of Lethington in her service and she herself would continue to hear Catholic Mass in her own apartments. Lord James would also support her claim to the English succession – an agreement hardly likely to endear him to his patron, Elizabeth I.

It is difficult to know at this distance what James' real feelings towards his half-sister were. She was, by all accounts, an attractive and charming woman and it seems likely that he would have been fond of her as his much younger sister. On the other hand he cannot but have been aware that, had matters gone differently in the 1530s his father might well have married his own mother and he would have been King of Scots. It can hardly be doubted that he thought he would make a better sovereign than the 18-year-old, French-educated, girl in front of him. His allegiance to the new religion was utterly sincere, and for that reason, too, he must have regretted that his sister was his rightful sovereign.

It appears that James' own friends were not completely certain of how he would react on seeing his sister. There were rumours that he might be offered the red hat of a Cardinal if he returned to the Catholic faith. He was still Prior of St Andrews, although he had never been ordained as a priest. Thomas Randolph assured Sir Nicholas Throckmorton that in fact Lord James's sights were set higher than a Cardinal's hat – he secretly coveted his sister's Crown. Randolph further undermined James' probity by saying that many believed that, rather than representing the interests of the Protestant party, Lord James was actually visiting his sister to obtain from her the Earldoms of Moray and Fife, and a leading position in the country, together with agreement to his marriage with Agnes Keith, daughter of the Earl Marischal.

From the imperfect knowledge that is the best we can have, perhaps the proper inference is that his primary allegiance was to his Protestant faith which he believed could be best maintained by alliance with England. If Mary would support the Protestant Reformation, then he would support her, but, if she would not, he would consider it legitimate to disobey her. On a darker note, it is possible he gave sanction to a rather unlikely scheme in which Mary would be granted a safe-conduct to travel through England, but would be abducted en route. Perhaps it was a knowledge of this secret plan that led Elizabeth to refuse a safe-conduct, obliging Mary to travel by sea, although it was assumed then, and subsequently, that the English Queen, offended by Mary's politically foolish claim in 1558 to be the rightful Queen of England, wished to make Mary's life difficult from the outset.

On his return to Scotland, James wrote a long letter to Mary, encouraging her to return to Scotland and giving advice on several points, the chief of which, was that she should not attempt to undo the work of the Reformation Parliament in establishing the Protestant religion. What he did not mention (although he had told Cecil about it) was that there was a strong faction of Catholics who had hoped to overturn the settlement. Throughout his advice to her, he gives the impression that anything contrary to what he and the Lords of the Congregation had established would be deeply injurious to her and to the good of the country. Whilst this was probably a completely genuine belief, his presentation of facts was one-sided.

He did, however, fulfil his promise to Mary to support her claim to be Elizabeth's heir in accordance with the usual English rules of inheritance. In very delicate terms he wrote to Elizabeth, pointing out that, if Mary were recognised as heir, after Elizabeth and any children she might have, this would satisfy Mary, removing a bone of contention between the two queens and leading to enhanced co-operation between the countries, to the good of the whole British Isles. His letter was in vain – he never received a response.

Chapter 9: The Return of the Queen

Although Maitland had been extremely fearful of the outcome of Mary arriving in Scotland, in late June she re-appointed him to royal service, writing candidly that she would forgive and forget the fact that he had been the chief instigator of the *'pratiques'* [plots or sinister practices] he and the Scottish nobles had entertained with England, if he would desist immediately from continuing them, and would arrange for the Scottish hostages, sent to England after the Treaty of Berwick, to be returned. She promised she would not listen to *'talebearers'* but that, if he served her loyally, she would treat him well. If, on the other hand, things went wrong, she would blame him, as he was the ring-leader amongst the Lords. Despite this olive branch, in August, Randolph wrote to Cecil that

James, Maitland, and their ally, the Earl of Morton, would all have preferred Mary to stay in France.

Maitland continued his treachery by writing to Cecil on 10 August informing him that James and he had been in the north, advancing religion, and that, should Mary return, it would be bad for the Protestant cause. He entreated Cecil to guard his letter carefully, and confirmed his commitment to keeping James and Chatelherault on good terms, for the Protestant cause in Scotland was dependent on their concord.

On 19 August 1561, Mary, Queen of Scots arrived in Leith after an absence of thirteen years from her homeland. Her arrival was swifter than anticipated, and few of her subjects were there to greet her. Only her half-brother, Lord Robert Stewart, was there to meet the Queen and her three Guise uncles who had accompanied her.

On hearing of her arrival, her other nobles hurried to meet her – first Chatelherault, then Lord James, followed by Chatelherault's son, Arran.

For the first five days after the Queen's arrival, no mention was made of religion. On the first Sunday, she heard Mass privately, with her own household and uncles, together with the Earl of Montrose and Lord Graham, with James and Lord Robert barring the door against those who objected. Lord Home stayed indoors, whilst the Protestant nobles went to hear Knox preaching his usual Sunday sermon.

The following day, Mary confirmed that she would make no attempt to change the religious settlement of the 1560 Parliament, but that she and her household would hear Mass in private.

It was immediately apparent that Mary intended to put her trust in Lord James and Maitland. She may genuinely have relied on her brother to support her, or she may have been playing a longer game, but for the first years of her personal rule, she gave every appearance of trusting

James and relying on his advice. Together with Maitland, Huntly, Atholl and Marischal, he was at the heart of her Council of sixteen.

James was still attempting to have the matter of the English succession confirmed – writing a reminder letter to Cecil to say he had not heard an answer to his proposal that Mary be confirmed as Elizabeth's heir.

As well as supporting Mary in this, he was soon obliged to comfort her following her first meeting with John Knox, which reduced her to tears. Knox had harangued her at great length, pointing out that idolatry (which he reckoned the Mass to be) had brought down plagues from God. She was sufficiently mistress of herself to suggest to him that he should not be so severe with people who disagreed with his opinions, and that he should 'use more meekness' in his sermons. He was assured that he could always speak freely from his conscience to her, and he agreed that he owed her obedience as a subject. Apparently, James stood by throughout the whole interview, saying nothing.

Nevertheless, Lord James was not happy with his sister's religion. Whilst her chaplains were singing a Mass on 14 September, he and his brother-in-law, Argyll, created a fracas resulting in fisticuffs. No-one in Scotland, including the Queen, seems to have been be particularly perturbed by this, demonstrating that violence even amongst the upper classes was endemic – it is hard to imagine a riot in Queen Elizabeth's chapel going unpunished!

Before long, Huntly and James, who were both advising Mary, quarrelled openly. Huntly claimed that, if Mary would but say the word, he would reinstitute the Catholic religion in his earldom, and James told him he would soon find himself mistaken in his power if he tried it (a vision of a couple of school boys comes to mind 'I can do x!', 'Yeah, right, you and whose army?', 'Mine, actually!') Rumours again surfaced that

James was less concerned about religion than he was about feathering his own nest.

Perhaps wishing to capitalise on James' good relations with England, he was dispatched in autumn 1561 as the Queen's Lieutenant, to keep peace in the Borders – attending a '*diet*' that is, one of the days set out for joint prosecution of malefactors from both sides. But whilst James was in favour with Mary, he had quarrelled with the Duke of Chatelherault and Arran, for some unknown cause.

The Duke was in bad odour with the Queen too, leaving court in a huff, because Mary intended to compel him to relinquish Dumbarton Castle. Dumbarton had been taken by Chatelherault by force from its rightful owner, the Earl of Lennox, but Chatelherault claimed that Marie of Guise had agreed he could keep it for 19 years, a period not due to end until 1566. Mary was talking of bringing Lennox back from England, which was anathema to Chatelherault and the other Hamiltons, as they had been in feud with Lennox Stewarts for years – Lennox believing he had a better claim to be Mary's heir in default of children. Lennox and James were also enemies, which, according to the English Ambassador, Randolph, lessened Lennox' chances of restoration.

Chapter 10: A Wife and Two Earldoms

In January 1562 Mary received Arran kindly at court and patched up some sort of reconciliation between the Hamiltons and James, and it was agreed that they would attend James' wedding. For, whilst the Hamiltons had lost Dumbarton, Mary was honouring James with the grant of two earldoms – Moray on 30 January 1562, and Mar on 7 February. The first grant was, initially, kept secret, but the second made a splendid present for his wedding the following day, Shrove Tuesday, to Agnes Keith, daughter of the Earl Marischal.

The ceremony was performed by John Knox, in the presence of the Queen, who was already fond of her new sister-in-law. Knox warned James in his sermon to be sure to continue his support of the Protestant Kirk, lest his new wife be blamed for any falling off of enthusiasm! The ceremony was followed by feasting and dancing at Holyrood, much to Knox's disgust, and the knighting of various of James' associates. James and Agnes had been betrothed for some years, and, as James was of age and in complete control of his destiny, we can assume that this was as close to a love-match as aristocratic marriages in the sixteenth century ever were.

The reason for secrecy over the grant of the Earldom of Moray was the slight technical hitch that Huntly, although not granted the title, had been administering the lands since 1549. It is hard to understand why Mary gave Moray the title – she must have known that Huntly would be provoked. There had been bad blood between Huntly and James for years, as noted above, and it is hard to avoid the conclusion that the new Earl of Moray was using his sister's trust in him to triumph over his enemy, who just happened to be the leading Catholic Earl.

Despite all of these quarrels and feuds – Huntly with James, James with the Lennox family (the Earl was still in England), the Lennoxes with the Hamiltons and the Hamiltons with the Earl of Bothwell, Mary endeavoured to keep the balance between them all, trying to keep the Crown above faction, but it was hard work.

During the spring of 1562, the Earl of Arran appeared to lose his mind. He had quarrelled, not for the first time, with James Hepburn, Earl of Bothwell (the background facts are a complex web of attacks, counter-attacks, cattle-raids, abductions and rescues – the usual

Borderers fare). Bothwell apologised handsomely and the two made up like long-lost brothers – a fact that surprised the Queen and her Council to such an extent that the Queen proposed to ride to Dumbarton to see what Arran and his father, the Duke, were up to. Arran later alleged that Bothwell had suggested that, in order to restore the Hamiltons to favour, Mary should be abducted en route by the two of them, whilst James and Maitland, who would, as a matter of course be with her, should be killed.

Apparently, Chatelherault was keen on the plan, but, he, Arran, suffering from a fit of conscience, confessed the matter to Mary and James and then told his father what he had done. Chatelherault was furious, and locked his son up, but Arran smuggled a letter out for James, before escaping from his room using his bedsheets! No sooner had James received the letter, whilst hunting with Mary, than another messenger raced up from Chatelherault, saying that Arran was making the whole story up.

Unsurprisingly, James and Mary did not know what to believe. Bothwell was sent for and locked up whilst the matter was investigated, and James went to see Arran, who was hiding out with William Kirkcaldy of Grange. Arran, was, by then, raving – talking of devils and witches, one of whom was, apparently, James' mother, Margaret Erskine. The next day, somewhat recovered, he was brought to Mary herself. By then, he seemed to be in his right mind, but said he would only confirm his story under certain conditions. The Queen rejected that idea immediately – he must either re-affirm what he had written in his letter to James, or confess he had made the whole thing up.

Chateleherault did not come to court, but said that his son was out of his mind – pointing out that Arran's mother and two aunts had also *been distempered with an unquiet humour*. Eventually, Arran retracted his allegations and seemed to be restored to health. Ambassador Randolph, nevertheless, did not entirely disbelieve the tale.

In August 1562, the first cracks in the relationship between James and Mary appeared. The Pope, Pius IV, sent a nuncio to visit Mary, in the hope that Scotland would send representatives to the reconvened Council of Trent. Mary, not wishing to aggravate her brother or the other Protestant lords, did not make much of the nuncio, but arranged with Maitland to meet him secretly whilst James and the others were attending Knox's sermon at St Giles. Long though Knox's perorations were, Mary mistook the time, and when James returned, he almost found them together. Mary made some excuse, but James was suspicious. Randolph thought that there was more to the visit than Mary had told Maitland, and he added that James might repent his decision not to allow the nuncio to be quietly murdered.

The dispute between the Hamiltons and James rumbled on, and it was suggested that Maitland should try to mediate – a united front between the Protestant Lords was considered important.

Chapter 11: The Overthrow of Huntly

Meanwhile, Huntly, who was at Inverness nursing a sore leg (if not wounded pride over the Earldom of Moray) was pleased to hear that his son, Lord John Gordon, had escaped from prison. Lord John was being held after wounding James, 5th Lord Ogilvy in a duel. This event may have contributed to Mary's desire to show her northern earl that the Crown was in charge, and must be obeyed. She decided to make a progress to the north of the country.

Mary, accompanied by James, Maitland, and the English Ambassador, Randolph, reached Aberdeen in mid-August, where they met Huntly and his Countess (who was the aunt of James' wife and reputed to indulge in witchcraft). Mary demanded that they return Lord John to imprisonment at Stirling, but Huntly dragged his feet whilst John, with a force of 1,000 horse, harried the Queen's train, and made no secret of the fact that he intended to abduct her.

The Queen showed her displeasure (and perhaps caution in the face of the threat of abduction) by refusing to visit Huntly at his main castle of Strathbogie. She was within four miles of the place when she turned back. This was a very severe mark of displeasure in a society where the sovereign's presence conferred power and prestige on her host. Instead, she headed for Darnaway Castle (once the home of James IV's mistress, Lady Janet Kennedy) and publicly announced the grant of the Earldom of Moray to James. James then resigned the Earldom of Mar to his cousin, Lord Erskine, who had a very good claim to it.

Moving on to Inverness, which was a royal castle, Mary's party was refused entry by the keeper, Lord Alexander Gordon, another of Huntly's sons. Despite Huntly's position as almost-King in the north, not all of his clan were prepared to support open treason, and he hurriedly sent a message to Lord Alexander to admit the Queen. In a show of authority, Mary had Alexander hanged from the castle battlements but John Gordon was still at large and threatening the Queen.

Mary, conferring with Moray (as we will now refer to James) decided to send for troops and commanded Huntly to prove his loyalty by surrendering the cannon he kept at Strathbogie.

Huntly was now in a cleft stick – he could give in and lose his power in the north, or he could rebel. He offered to help Mary track down his son John, provided he could bring his own troops, but the Queen was too cautious to believe that that would end well.

Egged on by Lady Huntly, the Earl finally marched towards the Queen with a force of around 1,000 men. He was confronted and vanquished by the royal army of some 2,000, led by Moray, together with the Earls of Atholl and Morton at the Battle of Corrichie on 25 October 1562. Huntly himself fell dead from his saddle, presumably of a stroke – he was a heavy, unhealthy man, although only in his late forties. In a ritual that makes modern stomachs turn, the Earl's embalmed body was sent south and, propped up in a chair, he was found guilty in Parliament of treason, in the presence of the Queen, and all his lands and titles were forfeited. Lord John was captured and hanged, also in front of the Queen, who was physically traumatised by the spectacle.

Moray came out of the affair very profitably – he received Huntly's sherriffdoms in Elgin, Inverness and Forres, and had dispatched one of the greatest threats to increased Protestant domination of Scotland.

By 1563, Mary was feeling confident in her rule. She had shown that she would not tolerate treason, by Catholics or Protestants, and she had kept her promise to accept the religious settlement of 1560. She had worked well with Moray and Maitland and won golden opinions from most people who met her. Moray himself could feel confident that his half-sister would continue to follow his advice, and that his path to increased riches and power would carry on smoothly. Alas for him, it became apparent over the following two years that Mary was only willing to accept Moray as her chief adviser so long as their interests aligned. Once her plans deviated from his, she would strike her own path, and would no more tolerate his disobedience, than she would that of Huntly.

Chapter 12: The Queen's Marriage

Moray had two goals – the promotion of Protestantism, best served by alliance with England, and his own power. For Mary, the preservation of good relations with England had been one of her guiding policies in the first years of her rule and her attempts to promote harmony between the two countries seem to have been genuine, although she still refused to ratify the Treaty of Edinburgh.

Mary's position was that she would ratify the Treaty, which proclaimed Elizabeth as the legitimate Queen of England (a point disputed by the Catholic powers of Europe in theory, if not in practice) if she herself were named as Elizabeth's heir. For practical purposes, Mary had completely accepted Elizabeth's position, wrote to her as Queen, and expressed herself in very respectful terms, almost as a younger sister, to her elder cousin. Mary was nine years younger than her cousin, and could hope to succeed to the wealthier, southern kingdom if her position were recognised. More practically, the Scottish Crown was poverty stricken, and could not afford any more wars with its neighbour.

Moray was deeply attached to the English alliance – it had afforded the means to implement the Reformation Parliament and remove the French troops, and it gave the Protestants a buttress in the shape of English cash and English arms, if Mary showed any signs of reneging on her promises to preserve the Reformation settlement. He pleaded with Elizabeth by personal letters, and also through Cecil, to confirm Mary's position, but to no avail. He also vigorously promoted the plan for the two Queens to meet. Mary was extremely eager for such a conference, but, although it was promised repeatedly, there was always some reason why Elizabeth could not confirm a definite date. As time went on, Mary became less and less trusting of Elizabeth's motives and words, and so it became more difficult to Moray to sustain the alliance.

Elizabeth was also making life difficult for Mary in relation to the latter's marriage. The Scottish Queen was told that, if she made a marriage that Elizabeth approved of, and refrained from any alliance the English did not like, she would be named as successor. Mary, who by 1563 had been a widow for three years and was eager to remarry to establish her own succession, was prepared to go along with this, but, although Elizabeth would tell her whom she could not marry, she refused to suggest a suitable candidate. Elizabeth vetoed Don Carlos, son of Philip II of Spain, and also the Archduke Charles of Austria. Eventually, having wasted (in Mary's view) another year, the English Queen, via Ambassador Randolph, suggested Lord Robert Dudley.

This was a bombshell, and a highly insulting one at that. Dudley was the son and grandson of men executed as traitors, the widower of a woman he was rumoured to have murdered, and such an intimate of Elizabeth herself as to be widely believed to be her lover. Mary was completely astonished and told Randolph she needed time to think it over. During the rest of 1564, Mary continued to secretly pursue a possible Spanish match, whilst Moray and Maitland ruminated over the advantages of a marriage to Dudley.

In November 1564, Moray, flanked by Maitland, met with the English Commissioners at Berwick to discuss the details of a marriage to Dudley (now promoted to the Earldom of Leicester to make him more palatable). They would be willing to encourage Mary to accept Leicester in return for a promise of the succession, but the English would not make a definite agreement. Moray told Cecil plainly that if the succession point were not clearly agreed, there could be no benefit for Mary in marrying Leicester, and she would turn her attention elsewhere.

In fact, there was already another contender. The Earl of Lennox, who had been exiled in England for twenty years, but returned to Scotland in late 1563 with Elizabeth's permission, had a son, Henry, Lord Darnley. Lord Darnley was a year or two younger than Mary – intelligent, well-educated and good looking. As well as having the disputed Lennox claim to be heir to the Scottish Crown, Darnley was also the next heir, after Mary herself, to the English Crown (according to strict primogeniture, although the waters had been muddied by Henry VIII's will, which excluded both Mary, and Darnley's mother, Lady Margaret Douglas). He had also been brought up Catholic, pleasing to Mary, but did not show any special enthusiasm for his religion, and might be willing to convert to Protestantism, pleasing to the Protestant Lords.

On his first appearance at the Scottish court, the young man seemed full of charm, and eagerness to please. He went to hear Knox preach, dined with Mary, Moray and Randolph and even danced galliards with the Queen at Moray's suggestion. Whilst the Queen at first seemed only to be considering Darnley for his claims to the English succession, after she nursed the young man through an attack of measles in April 1565, she fell so far in love (or lust) with him that she made up her mind to marry him.

Chapter 13: The Chaseabout Raid

Moray was deeply disturbed by Mary's choice. For four years he had been his half-sister's most important adviser, and any husband would be likely to have ousted him. Added to that, the English took umbrage at Mary's choice (although many people then, and now, believed that Elizabeth had engineered it because she knew Darnley would prove a disastrous match). Moray could see that his long-term alliance with England might be under threat. There was Darnley's own character – vain, spoilt, spiteful (as everyone but the Queen had observed) and ambitious for power himself – he had already told people that he believed Moray had too much influence and power. Finally, there was his position as a member of the Lennox family – whom Moray considered his enemies.

Once it became apparent that Mary was fixed on the marriage, Moray withdrew from court – ostensibly to avoid any Catholic ceremonies he might be obliged to witness at Easter, and at the end of June he remained at his half-brother, Sir William Douglas' Castle of Lochleven, rather than attending the Queen at Perth with the other nobles.

On 1 July, even before Mary had actually married Darnley (which took place on 29 July 1565), Moray wrote to Ambassador Randolph, requesting £3,000 to be sent by England to support the Protestant faith – presumably through armed rebellion. Moray was not alone, but Mary had enough support from the other Protestant Lords to show that Moray was merely using religion as a cloak for rebellion. Moray was summoned to the royal presence to explain himself. He was offered a safe-conduct for himself and a retinue of eighty. He refused to come and, on 6 August, was '*put to the horn*' (the term for being outlawed – announced by three blasts of a horn). Chatelherault and Argyll (brother-in-law to Mary and Moray) were told in no uncertain terms that they were not to help him, or they would find themselves on the wrong side of the law as well. They both chose to ignore her orders.

Moray's lands were declared forfeit (although an act of Parliament would be required to actually confiscate them) and Mary mustered troops at Edinburgh to march against him – pawning her jewels to raise the necessary money. Mary reiterated her commitment to the settlement of

1560 to make it clear she was punishing rebellion, not attempting to impose religious changes. She marched out of Edinburgh at the head of her army on 26 August, heading for Glasgow and Argyll's lands. No sooner had she left, than Moray, together with the Lords Rothes, Glencairn and Chatelherault, entered the city. They were soon dismayed to discover they had no support. Mary was popular, and her confirmation of the religious settlement meant that no-one was interested in overthrowing her. Even Moray's cousin, Erskine, to whom he had ceded the Earldom of Mar, supported the Queen. To ensure further support, Mary pardoned Huntly's eldest son, restoring his Earldom, and brought the Earl of Bothwell (a notorious enemy of Moray) back into the fold of royal favour. Even Moray's friend, James Douglas, Earl of Morton, was reconciled to the royal marriage when Darnley's mother gave up her claim to the Douglas Earldom of Angus to him.

Mary and Darnley pursued Moray and his allies in what became known as the 'Chaseabout Raid' as the royal and rebel armies marched hither and yon across the south of Scotland without ever coming to blows.

Moray requested help from England. Although fine words were spoken, and Elizabeth had written to Mary in July requesting her to take Moray back into favour (even though the tone of the letter was hardly likely to promote the request), the English Queen would not openly support rebels. She would go no further than offering Moray sanctuary in England. On 6 October, Moray crossed into England. He felt aggrieved at the lack of support, writing to Leicester and Cecil that he and his colleagues would not have taken the action they had, without Elizabeth's more-than-tacit support - in fact, actual letters from Elizabeth's Council.

He travelled to London to plead in person with Elizabeth but she, keen to demonstrate her solidarity with fellow-monarchs and discourage rebellion, first made him wait at Royston (about 30 miles north of London) then gave him a public dressing-down, in front of the French Ambassador. Nevertheless, she permitted him to take up residence in Newcastle, and promised to write again to Mary, requesting he be forgiven. Moray remained in Newcastle throughout the autumn and winter of 1565-1566 with no sign of forgiveness from his half-sister. Mary was angry, hurt, and probably shocked, at what she perceived to be Moray's astounding ingratitude. She had given him wealth, power, position and trust, and he had repaid her by trying to control her, and prevent her marriage.

Chapter 14: Assassination

No matter whom Mary had chosen to marry, there would have been difficulties with England, with her courtiers and with Moray, but Darnley's own character, which quickly became apparent to everyone, including the Queen, was a greater hindrance to the success of the match than any displeasure of her nobles.

By October 1565, the honeymoon had already worn off, and the two were quarrelling. In particular, they argued over who should be Lieutenant in the Borders – a role previously filled by Moray. Mary wished to appoint the Earl of Bothwell, whilst Darnley argued for his father, Lennox, to receive the commission. Nevertheless, Darnley had completed at least part of his side of the bargain, and by December it was known that Mary was pregnant.

Mary, having had every success in 1565, was unaware of the troubles about to mount up on multiple fronts. Flexing her new-found muscles and determined to deal with Moray and the rest of the rebels, she summoned a Parliament for spring 1566, with a view to putting the forfeit of their lands into practice. Knox and other Protestants were worried that she would use the Parliament to promote a more Catholic agenda. At the same time, Darnley, angry that he was not King in fact, as well as name, began to believe himself ill-done-by.

Moray and his confederates soon saw that Darnley was a loose cannon and that they could attack Mary through him. Having objected to the Queen marrying him, on the grounds both that he was Catholic, and that it would stir up dissension, by February 1566, they were insinuating to him, that, in fact, it would be better for him to be King, rather than just the Queen's husband. They also worked upon Darnley's jealousy of Mary's Italian secretary, David Riccio, whom they suggested was actually her lover, and perhaps the father of the coming child. This is most unlikely, as, quite apart from the fact that Mary behaved at all times with the utmost propriety, it would have meant her having an affair with Riccio in the very months when she was most infatuated with Darnley.

An agreement was drawn up between the conspirators to obtain the Crown Matrimonial for Darnley (this would have given him equality with Mary during her life, and he would have retained the Crown on her death). Moray signed the bond on 2 March 1566 whilst still in Newcastle, along with the Earls of Morton, Argyll, Rothes and Glencairn and Lords Lindsay, Boyd and others. Naturally, no mention was made of the plan to assassinate Riccio, although that was the actual purpose of the conspiracy – Moray and the rest had no intention of bestowing power on Darnley.

It was imperative that action be taken before the Queen persuaded Parliament to forfeit Moray's and the other rebels' lands – a debate scheduled for 12 March.

The fullness of the plan was well-known in London, Randolph informing Cecil on 9 March that Darnley intended

'To take away this occasion of slander he [Darnley] is himself determined to be at the apprehension and execution of him, whom he is able manifestly to charge with the crime and to have done him the most dishonour that can be to any man.'

On the very same day, Darnley, Ruthven, Morton and others burst into Mary's apartments where she was dining with her friends and Riccio, dragged the screaming secretary out, and butchered him within earshot of the Queen, who was held by Darnley with Ruthven's pistol pointed at her pregnant belly.

In a triumph of quick-thinking and charm, Mary persuaded Darnley to desert his conspirators – pointing out that they would soon abandon him and they laid a plan to escape from Edinburgh. Unaware that Moray had been involved, when he arrived on the 11 March, Mary threw herself into his arms and cried *'Oh, my brother, if you had been here, they would not have used me thus.'* Moray merely treated his sister to a sermon on the benefits of mercy, to which she replied that she had had plenty of practice in that, since coming to Scotland. Early the next morning, aided by Bothwell and Huntly, Mary and Darnley crept out of Edinburgh Castle and rode twenty-five miles in the dark, to the safety of Dunbar Castle.

Mary, remaining unaware of Moray's involvement in Riccio's death, pardoned him, Glencairn and Argyll for the actions that had led to the Chaseabout Raid – she was far more determined to pursue those whom she knew to be responsible for Riccio's death. The new outlaws (Morton,

Ruthven and the rest) wrote to Moray that he should not forgo the opportunity to be taken back into favour on their account. He also received the welcome sum of £1,000 from Queen Elizabeth as well as admonitions to be faithful to his sovereign – presumably less welcome. He and his fellow conspirators complained to Randolph that Darnley had not kept his word to them, and was seeking to have his fellow conspirators punished, whilst he was restored to the Queen's side. By April, however, Mary had seen the bond that had been signed and knew the full guilt of Darnley and the others.

Determined to overcome factions in preparation for the birth of her child, Mary sought reconciliation between Moray, Glencairn and Argyll, and the men who were previously their enemies, Atholl, Huntly and Bothwell. On the surface, she achieved her desire – they swallowed their differences and the six of them formed the core of her Privy Council – two Catholics (Atholl and Huntly) and the rest Protestant. However, the Queen was hard put to conceal her anger and contempt for her husband.

Chapter 15: Planning a Murder

On 16 June, Mary bore a son, named James, and Moray wrote letters to Elizabeth and Cecil, requesting that a high-ranking personage be sent to attend the baptism as proxy for Elizabeth who was to be god-mother. He was still hoping to promote a long-term alliance between the two countries.

Following the Prince's birth, the Queen was in poor health, and her relationship with Darnley was deteriorating further, they quarrelled publicly, and he was often the worse for drink.

Despite the apparent reconciliation between the Lords, Bothwell and Moray were still on bad terms – in particular, Moray wanted Maitland to be pardoned for his part in the Riccio affair (he had not signed the bond, yet had been banished to Flanders). Bothwell wanted Maitland kept out of the country. Mary agreed that Maitland should come into her presence and that he, Moray and Bothwell should thrash the matter out. This was done in September 1566, and Bothwell and Maitland were apparently reconciled. Later that month, there was another public confrontation between Mary and her husband. Darnley had complained that he was so ill-treated by his wife, and accorded such little respect, that he was determined to leave the country. In front of her Council, Mary asked him to state his grievances, but he did not come up with anything concrete and left the room.

Bothwell now came to be the most trusted of Mary's advisers – perhaps because he was the only one who had not betrayed her, but there was no talk of there being any relationship between them other than of sovereign and councillor.

During the autumn, Moray accompanied Mary on a Justice in Eyre, to be held at Jedburgh. Whilst they were there, news came that Bothwell had fallen ill. A few days later, the whole court visited him in his sickbed, returning the same day. Once back at Jedburgh, Mary collapsed into serious illness – possibly a ruptured ulcer. She lay sick for weeks, and at one point was believed to have died, before regaining consciousness. On what she herself thought was her deathbed, she left her son her kingdom, specifically excluding Darnley. She also begged Moray (whom she presumably intended to act as Regent) to promise that, as she had not attempted to interfere with Protestants, so he should not interfere with Catholics.

Mary recovered, but the whole kingdom was left with the problem of Darnley and pretty much everyone, except his father, Lennox, wanted to see the back of him – preferably permanently.

According to the depositions of Huntly and Argyll, made two years later, they, together with Moray, Maitland and Bothwell, had agreed that they should find a way to arrange a divorce for Mary. Maitland informed Mary of their ideas, and she agreed that, provided a divorce would not impugn the legitimacy of her son, or harm her honour, that that would be the best course. In order to secure their support, Mary was to agree to the reinstatement of the Earl of Morton, still exiled for his part in the murder of Riccio. This agreement is known as the Craigmillar Bond. Although there is no contemporary copy of it, it was referred to as having existed by some of the signatories.

Other reports suggest that there was more to the Bond, and that both Moray and Mary (or only one of them depending on the viewpoint of the commentator) knew that divorce was not the real plan, but murder. In this case, either or both 'looked through their fingers' – that is, chose not to understand the implications of the Bond. There were certainly rumours that something was afoot – on 18 January 1567, the Spanish Ambassador in London wrote to Philip of Spain that Mary had been approached to join a plot to murder her husband, but had declined.

What happened next has been argued over for centuries, so we are unlikely to uncover the truth here. The facts are that Darnley, who had been ill, was visited by Mary who appeared to be attempting a reconciliation. He was brought to Edinburgh and lodged in a house at Kirk o'Fields where Mary spent considerable time nursing him until it was pronounced that he would be well enough to return to normal life at court on the following day – 10 February 1567.

Moray left Edinburgh on the morning of 9 February, informing his half-sister that he needed to visit Lady Moray who had suffered a miscarriage. The same night, Mary and several of the Lords, including Bothwell, Argyll, Huntly and Cassilils visited Darnley, had dinner and played the usual gambling games. Late in the evening Mary and the courtiers left to attend a wedding party. At around three in the morning, an explosion was heard. The house at Kirk o'Fields was blown up, but Darnley's body, rather than being found in the wreckage, was found in the garden in his nightshirt, with no mark of the blast on him and was presumed, therefore, to have been suffocated.

The Queen and Council wrote to the monarchs of Europe, informing them of the dreadful event, which, they said, had actually been aimed at Mary herself – only the lucky fact of her having left to go to the wedding feast had saved her. Every effort would be made to bring the perpetrators to justice.

Chapter 16: Accusations

Within days rumours were circulating that Bothwell had been behind the murder, aided by Morton and one of Bothwell's confederates, Sir James Balfour. Very quickly it was suggested that Mary had been party to it. Abroad, it was rumoured that all of the nobles had been involved, including Moray, whom the Ambassador to Savoy named particularly as having quarrelled with Darnley.

Robert Stedall, in his *The Survival of the Crown*, goes further than most historians in planting the blame for Darnley's death squarely at Moray's door, aided by Cecil. Their motive, he alleges, was for Moray to gain control of Scotland as Regent for the baby James, so that any risk of

Catholic resurgence under Mary either in Scotland, or, after her probable succession to the English throne, could be eliminated. According to Stedall, Bothwell was to be hoodwinked into arranging Darnley's murder, investigated in a perfunctory fashion and exonerated, and that Mary would then be persuaded to marry Bothwell, which would lead everyone to assume they had colluded and were both guilty of murder. This is, of course, exactly what happened, but given the complexities of the situation, the way events unfolded and the different courses that Mary might have taken throughout, it is rather hard to swallow that Moray could have planned it all in advance – although if anyone could, it was Cecil!

Moray, keen to disassociate himself from the whole affair, either because he was guilty, or because he genuinely thought his sister guilty, left Scotland almost immediately. He wrote on 13 March to Cecil, thanking the latter for *'the many and large benefits'* he had received from him and requesting an immediate passport to travel through England. The fact that he left his daughter to the guardianship of Mary does not accord with him viewing her as a cold-blooded murderer.

Moray travelled to France where he remained for the next six months. There is no information as to exactly what he did or where he went. In May, Sir William Kirkcaldy of Grange, requested him to return, but either he never received the request, or decided to stay away. In July, by which time Mary had been, effectively, deposed and was being held in captivity at Lochleven, Moray's half-brother's castle, Moray's messenger, carrying letters to Mary, went to Elizabeth, presumably under Moray's instructions. Moray's orders had been to give the letters directly into Mary's hands and not into those of the Lords holding her. The messenger was to tell the Lords that he *'misliked'* their holding the Queen in *'durance'*. He was also to assure Mary of his loyalty.

Elizabeth sent further messages to Mary – she was to understand that Moray had never accused her of Darnley's murder, never planned to abduct Prince James, and that, far from being in league against her, Moray was her most faithful servant. All of these admonitions from Elizabeth suggest that Mary believed quite the opposite.

On 24 July 1567, having miscarried twins and being physically intimidated by Lord Lindsay, Mary was coerced into abdication. Five days later, her son, James, was crowned as James VI, and it was agreed that Moray should be Regent.

In early August, Moray returned and was received very enthusiastically by the people of Edinburgh. He visited Mary at Lochleven, and they quarrelled bitterly. Whilst he did not accuse her of murdering Darnley, he said that her people were dissatisfied with her, and that her marriage to Bothwell had brought her into disrepute. It was not enough that she might be innocent in God's eyes, she should also have the appearance of innocence. He probably threatened that she would be executed, as she spent the night in a state of fear and anguish.

The next day, he promised her that he would save her life, and told her that with him as Regent she would be safer than with anyone else in that role. He claimed that she capitulated and asked him to undertake the Regency, although she also pointed out to him that, if men would rebel against their lawful sovereign, they would have no problem breaking their faith to him.

Moray was officially proclaimed Regent on 22 August, although he cried crocodile tears to Cecil in a letter of 30 August, in which he claimed to have had no desire at all for the position, but hoped he might be able to serve Mary and James in that role. He compensated himself for the pain of his position by taking Mary's jewels. Some he gave to his wife, and others, he later sold to Elizabeth, including a famous string of pearls.

This act of appropriation *'colded'* the stomachs of the Hamiltons, who had been ambivalent about Mary's deposition.

Whilst Cecil was jubilant, Elizabeth was not. As the Earl of Leicester wrote,

'The Queen takes the doings of these Lords to heart, as a precedent most perilous for any Prince'

Yet, if Moray were going to be Regent anyway, it was better for him to be positively disposed towards her than towards France. The French government had already given Moray a pension of 1,500 crowns as well as a handsome cash present before his return to Scotland and it was clear that if the French could renew their traditional alliance with a Scotland ruled by Moray, they did not care too much about the fate of Mary. Moray was well aware that Elizabeth's public condemnation was not necessarily indicative of the true state of her feelings. He wrote to Cecil:

'Although the Queen's Majesty, your mistress, outwardly seem not altogether to allow the present state here, yet doubt I not that Her Highness in her heart likes it well enough.'

Chapter 17: Mary's Escape

In the autumn of 1567, Moray occupied himself in the Borders and in the punishment of those who were to take the blame for Darnley's death – Bothwell's associates. No blame was attached to any of the others who had been involved in the Craigmillar Bond. Even the man who was widely known to have been the prime mover in the affair, Sir James Balfour, was pardoned and granted lands and money from Moray's own estates. Moray also tried to come to terms with the Hamiltons, who were pressing for Mary's release.

By and large, Moray's rule was accepted. He was effective in the Borders and his suppression of Catholicism gained plaudits from the more radical Protestants. A crack appeared when he quarrelled with his long term friend and supporter, the Earl of Argyll. Argyll and his wife, Lady Jean Stewart, who was Moray's half-sister, had been miserable together for years, but Moray would not agree to them being divorced. Argyll left the Regent and joined the Hamiltons, holding out at Dumbarton Castle.

In December, Moray called a Parliament at which Mary, for the first time, was accused of complicity in Darnley's murder. A letter substantiating the claim was talked of, but not produced. Mary's capacity as an adult, which had been confirmed by an Act of 1564 was reaffirmed, to prevent the revocation of any acts made before her twenty-fifth birthday. Under normal Scottish practice, any acts made by a monarch before he or she was twenty-five could be rescinded, and this tradition might be used to invalidate either her abdication or her previous grants of land and office. Some of the nobles, including Huntly and Herries, refused to sign the Act of Abdication which confirmed that Mary was no longer Queen, and that James VI was now King, with Moray as Regent.

Mary's appeal to Moray to appear and defend herself was ignored. The undertakings of Parliament were reported in person to Mary at Lochleven by Moray, Morton and Sir James Balfour. Presumably the irony of the situation was not lost on any of them – they had taken her Crown for a crime that they are far more likely to have committed than she (although it is hard to believe that Mary had no inkling of the plot against Darnley).

All was not straightforward for Moray. There were plenty of people who believed that the murder of Darnley had been perpetrated not by Bothwell alone, but by Moray, Morton, Maitland and the other Lords who had met at Craigmillar. This was confirmed when John Hay of Tallo, executed for some part in the assassination, yelled out the names of Huntly, Argyll, Balfour and Maitland from the scaffold, as partakers in the Bond.

Maitland seems, surprisingly, to have been pricked by his conscience – or else he was concerned that Mary's abdication under duress was illegal, which would endanger his position. Despite having been Moray's ally for years, he was now barred from the Council, suspected by Moray of sympathy for the Queen, and, indeed, he began sending secret message to Mary.

The Hamiltons, too, believing that Moray was after the throne himself, which would remove their status as the legitimate heirs, withdrew their support.

In May 1568, Moray was 'sore amazed' to hear that Mary had escaped from Lochleven. With the support of Argyll, Huntly, Maxwell and others, she raised a formidable army, significantly outnumbering Moray's troops. The two forces met at Langside, but, despite superiority of numbers, Mary's army was less well-disciplined and fell into disarray when Argyll was suddenly incapacitated – possibly from a stroke or fit. Moray's troops triumphed, and Mary, rejecting better advice, crossed the Solway Firth, to a lifetime of imprisonment in England.

Elizabeth was aghast at the problem confronting her. To commit to helping Mary regain her throne would reinstate a Catholic Queen and encourage her hopes of succession and the many Catholics still in England. To refuse aid would give succour to rebels against a crowned sovereign. If she did neither, holding Mary without any valid reason, she might expose England to attack from France or Spain.

Moray was urging that Mary be kept under lock and key, denouncing her for murder and adultery and asking for assurance that, if he could prove the Queen guilty by her own letters, she would be held in England. It is not hard to infer from Moray's letter, that, if he were assured Mary would be held, he would find the evidence.

'For what purpose shall we either accuse, or take care how to prove, when we are not assured what to prove, or, when we have proved, what shall succeed?'

Elizabeth temporised, claiming to Mary that she could not help her until Mary's innocence had been proven, meanwhile, she wrote to Moray, assuring him that, no matter what Elizabeth might say publically, she would not help Mary to be restored to the throne.

Chapter 18: York Commission

A Commission was summoned to try Mary at York.   In early September, Moray sent the documents now known as the Casket Letters, to Cecil.   These letters, widely believed now to be forgeries, and little regarded by the English Commissioners at the time, purported to show, via correspondence between Mary and Bothwell, that they had had an affair before Darnley's death, and conspired to murder him.   They had not been produced previously, during Mary's imprisonment at Lochleven, and only one had been referred to, but not produced in the December Parliament which had confirmed her abdication. (For a full discussion of the letters, see Antonia Fraser's *'Mary Queen of Scots'* or John Guy's *'My Heart is My Own'*).

Moray attended the Commission, which opened on 4 October 1568, in person, together with Morton, Maitland and three secretaries. It was to be presided over by the English Duke of Norfolk, assisted by the Earl of Sussex and Sir Ralph Sadler. Before submitting to the Commission's authority, Moray requested that a judgement would be made on Mary's guilt, and if it were proven, Elizabeth would not do anything to restore Mary to the throne. He was given the reassurance he sought. Before the formal proceedings began, Moray amused himself by travelling around Yorkshire – visiting Beverly, Hull and Pontefract, where Sussex arranged for him to be well received.

Mary, at first, planned to attend herself, but changed her mind when she finally understood that, far from the Commission having been set up to enquire into why Moray and the others had rebelled against her and deposed her, it was to be a trial of her alleged involvement in Darnley's death. Refusing to be tried by an English court, she decided to send Commissioners in her stead – this was all to the good as far as her enemies were concerned. The last thing they needed was Mary disputing manufactured evidence in front of people who might, just possibly, be impartial.

The Commission proceeded, being removed to London at the end of the month. It was soon apparent, however, that no real trial could possibly be welcome to any of the participants. If Mary were shown to be innocent, then Moray and the rest would be condemned as forgers, and Elizabeth would have little option but to help Mary back to her throne. If Mary were found guilty, then Elizabeth would be obliged to hand her back to Scotland, where she would certainly be executed – not an option that was at all palatable to a fellow monarch. So a sordid compromise was reached between the English and Scottish governments. Mary's name would be so thoroughly besmirched, without her ever being able to defend herself, that Elizabeth would be justified in keeping her in captivity, but not obliged to hand her over to certain death.

Moray and Morton testified, and produced the Casket Letters, but Mary was not permitted to appear and, when her representatives finally protested the illegality of the proceedings, they were ignored. Eventually, on 11 January 1569, the Commission was dismissed. The verdict was that the Scottish Lords had not proved that Queen Mary was guilty of any crimes, but nor had any evidence been shown to convict the Lords of rebellion. Moray, Morton and the rest travelled back to Scotland, Moray with the sweet sound of £5,000 jingling in his saddlebags and the Casket Letters rustling in their snug silver box. Mary remained incarcerated.

Moray now settled down to the business of being Regent, but his path was not smooth. From initially acquiescing in the Queen's deposition, enough of her subjects, particularly the Hamiltons (Chatelherault and his sons and family), Huntly, Herries and Maxwell formed what became known as the Queen's Party, in opposition to the King's Party. At the very least they wanted Mary nominally restored as Queen, perhaps in joint rule with her son. There were constant disturbances and Moray spent much of 1569 riding around the country to suppress rebellions led by the Queen's supporters.

A match had been suggested between the English Duke of Norfolk, a Protestant, and Mary. Initially, Moray seemed to favour the idea, until he concluded that such a match, even if the plan was, ostensibly, that Mary should stay in England, was unlikely to end well for him. When the Kirk Convention, held on 25 July, 1569, was asked to approve a divorce between Bothwell and Mary (who had been married according to Protestant rites), he refused to approve it, and carried the majority of the Convention with him. Voting in favour of the divorce were Moray's former allies, Argyll, Maitland and Balfour. Furious at this betrayal,

Moray ordered Maitland's arrest on the grounds of involvement in Darnley's death, sending him to Edinburgh Castle, held by Sir William Kirkcaldy of Grange, who, unknown to Moray at this juncture, was also looking for the restoration of the Queen. But Maitland knew too much, and Moray did not proceed with a trial.

In late December 1569, Moray tried to overcome the Queen's Party, which still held the impregnable fortress of Dumbarton, under the captaincy of Lord Fleming. Fleming and the Hamilton brothers – Lords John and Claud – despite being offered immunity from prosecution if they surrendered, held out. They had another plan – nothing less than the assassination of the Regent.

A member of the Hamilton clan, Sir James Hamilton of Bothwellhaugh was chosen to do the deed. He had a personal grudge against Moray, as, following the Battle of Langside, where he had been a captain in the Queen's army, his lands had been forfeited. Armed with a carbine (an early handgun), he followed Moray as the Regent travelled back from Dumbarton to Linlithgow. Hamilton spent the night in the Archbishop's house, then, as Moray passed by on horseback, shot him from an upstairs window.

The bullet hit Moray in the abdomen, but did not kill him immediately. Dismounting, he walked back to his lodging, but his condition deteriorated and he died that night. The date is variously given as the 21 or 23 January, 1570.

Hamilton made good his escape, and spent the rest of his life in France, granted a pension by Mary, who said she was indebted to him, although she had not instigated the act.

Moray's body was taken to Holyrood Palace in Edinburgh. His coffin was then carried by the men who had supported him throughout his career – Morton, Lindsay, Glamis, Ruthven and others - to St Giles

Cathedral. His mother, Margaret Erskine, Lady Douglas, also attended the funeral. Despite disapproving of excessive funeral orations, Knox made an exception in this case, and preached a sermon which moved the congregation of some three thousand to tears for the loss of their *'good and godly'* Regent. Scotland descended into faction fighting that was little better than civil war.

Moray left a widow and three daughters (one not born until after his death). The eldest, Lady Elizabeth Stewart, inherited her father's earldom. Lady Moray remarried within eighteen months of Moray's death – to the brother, and heir, of Moray's erstwhile ally, the Earl of Argyll. She pursued a long and acrimonious battle with the Scottish government for reimbursement of the costs Moray had defrayed whilst Regent.

Conclusion

Sir James Melville, from whose Memoirs much of the detail of the period is known, and who was a friend and supporter of Moray all his life, described him as *'good with good company, wise with wise company, stout with stout company, and contrariwise with others of contrary qualities.'*

This is a more understanding portrait of him, than perhaps can be supported by all the evidence. Whether or not Moray was complicit in the murder of Darnley, and the evidence against him is not much stronger than the evidence against Mary, he was undoubtedly a party to the assassination of Riccio, and despite his protestations about loyalty to Mary, this loyalty never extended to doing anything contrary to his own interests. He might well have made an effective King of Scots, had his parents been married, and he does not seem to have indulged in the personal violence that Bothwell, Morton, Ruthven and some of the other

Lords freely took part in and even, ironically, had prevented a death sentence being pronounced after the Battle of Langside on the man who would eventually assassinate him, yet, whilst he liked to keep his hands clean, he was glad enough to take advantage of others' misdeeds to obtain power for himself.

Part 2: Aspects of Moray's Life

Chapter 19: Following the Footsteps of James, Earl of Moray

Whilst Moray spent the majority of his life in lowland Scotland, he also travelled to the north-east of the country and made at least two journeys to France and several to England, sometimes on diplomatic missions, but also as an exile.

The numbers in the article below correspond to those on the map which follows.

*

Lord James Stewart, the Earl of Moray was born at the Castle of Dunnottar (1), one of the most spectacular ruins in Scotland, situated about two miles south of Stonehaven in Aberdeenshire. Overlooking the sea, it is almost impregnable mediaeval fortress. Quite why James was born here is unclear, as his mother was Margaret Erskine, Lady Douglas, and the Castle was in the possession of the Keith family, the Earls Marischal. It's possible that Lady Margaret was visiting with James V, who was definitely there in 1531 (the likely year of James' birth) exempting Marischal and his men from certain types of military service.

James V was happy to recognise his numerous illegitimate children and Moray and his half-siblings spent time in all of the royal palaces, including the Palace of Holyroodhouse (2) in Edinburgh. Holyrood, which was extensively remodelled by James V is today, Her Majesty The Queen's official residence in Scotland. In the heart of Edinburgh, it is well worth visiting. It was at Holyrood that Lord James was married in 1562, to Lady Agnes Keith, daughter of the Earl Marischal and granted the Earldoms of Mar and Moray. It was also at Holyrood that the murder of David Riccio took place, an event that Murray almost certainly knew was going to occur.

Although in the lower ranks of society people did not generally travel huge distances, amongst the upper classes in Scotland, travel to France and other European countries was frequent. Moray may well have attended university in Paris for a short period, after delivering his half-sister to the French court in 1548. He also visited France in the train of Marie of Guise on her visit to Mary Queen of Scots in 1550 - 1551. The party returned via England and it is probably at Westminster (3) or Whitehall that Moray first became acquainted with some of the leading lights of the Protestant court of Edward VI. These men would later become his allies - Sir William Cecil, later chief Secretary of State to Elizabeth I, Sir Henry Killigrew, and others. Even more importantly, one of the chaplains at the English court was the Scotsman, John Knox, who was breathing a radical version of Protestantism into the upper echelons of English society. Moray was distinctly impressed by him. The Tudor Palace of Whitehall has now disappeared, as has the mediaeval Palace of Westminster. The only exception is the 14th century Westminster Hall which still forms part of the Houses of Parliament and can be visited as part of a guided tour.

Lord James, and others, impressed with what he had seen of John Knox, invited him to return to Scotland. It was at Perth (4) that Knox began to attract large crowds, keen to hear his new doctrines as he preached in the Kirk of St John. His inflammatory denunciation of idolatry gave rise to rioting in the town, and widespread destruction of Catholic places of worship. Lord James, although becoming increasingly attached to the Protestant faith, was still working with his stepmother Marie of Guise and tried to quell the disturbances, but to no avail.

Relationships between Queen Marie and the Lords of the Congregation now deteriorated. Lord James formally joined the Protestant Lords and led an army which captured Stirling Castle (5). Stirling was one of the most important strongholds in Scotland, guarding the crossing of the Firth of forth. Two of the most important battles in Scottish history were fought beneath its walls – Bannockburn and Sauchieburn. It's a stunning place to visit, the great Hall of James IV and the Palace block built by James V have been extensively restored and the Palace block, in particular, has been decorated as it would have been during the Regency of Marie of Guise.

On Marie's death, Lord James travelled to France to understand his half-sister Mary Queen of Scots' plans for returning to Scotland. Having met with her, and formed the basis of a good working relationship, he showed his allegiance to the Protestant faith to be more important to him than his loyalty to his sovereign. On his return to Scotland he visited England again to inform Elizabeth I and Sir William Cecil of his discussions with Mary.

Nevertheless during the first couple of years of Mary's personal rule, Lord James was always at her side. In 1562, she granted in the title of Earl of Moray, and he was at her side during her expedition to the North of Scotland, aimed at taming the power of George Gordon, 4th Earl of Huntly. Moray was at Inverness Castle (6) when the keeper of it, Sir Alexander Gordon, refused to allow the Queen to enter. The insubordination of the Gordons was soundly punished when Murray led the Queen's troops to a decisive victory at the Battle of Corrichie (7), which took place near Meikle Tap in Aberdeenshire. There is a commemorative plaque on the site of the battlefield.

Moray's relationship with his half-sister deteriorated when he objected to her marriage to Lord Darnley. Following the Chaseabout

Raid in 1565, during which the Queen's forces scattered those of Moray and his colleagues, Moray was forced into exile in England. He spent some six months in Newcastle (8), although where exactly he lived is unknown. In his absence, although with his knowledge, a number of the Lords, led by Darnley, decided to assassinate the Queen's secretary, David Riccio. Murray arrived back at Holyroodhouse the following day. Mary does not seem to have asked how he came to appear so quickly.

Apparently reconciled with Mary, Moray was with her while she conducted a justice in Eyre based at Jedburgh (9). He remained with her whilst she lay there bedridden and close to death. It has been alleged that Moray was aware of the Bond of Craigmillar, which probably envisaged the death of Darnley, however there is no definite proof.

Within a few weeks of Darnley's assassination, Moray left for France. According to some accounts this was without Mary's permission, but other records say she gave consent. He returned to see his sister in her prison at Lochleven (10), where they quarrelled bitterly. The Queen, having been forced to abdicate, Moray became Regent and led the troops loyal to the new King, James VI, at Langside (11) when Mary was finally defeated. Once the Queen was in England, Moray made a number of attempts to have her returned to Scotland, however, Queen Elizabeth was reluctant to permit this, fearing she would executed. In the autumn of 1568, Moray travelled to York (12) to attend a Commission set up by Elizabeth I to investigate the circumstances of Mary's deposition. Mary was convinced that the Commission was being set up to enquire into why Moray and the others had rebelled, whilst Moray had been assured that it would investigate the Queen's alleged involvement in the murder of Darnley. The Commission was transferred from York to London to Westminster (3) and Hampton Court.

On his return to Scotland, Moray attempted to deal with the remaining members of the Queen's Party. In particular he hoped to drive her supporters, headed by John, 5th Lord Fleming, out of Dumbarton Castle (13), which he besieged. It soon became apparent that the Castle could not be captured, it having been relieved by supplies from a French ship. Moray withdrew, and on his return to Edinburgh broke his journey at Linlithgow (14).

He did not stay in the beautiful Palace of Linlithgow, the haunting ruins of which may still be visited, but in a private lodging. Setting out from Linlithgow on either the 21 or 23 January 1570, Murray was shot and killed by Sir James Hamilton of Bothwellhaugh. He died later that day and his body was conveyed to Edinburgh where it was interred in the south aisle of High Kirk of St Giles (15) on Tuesday, 14 February, 1570.

A monument was erected at a cost of £133 6s 8d, with a brass plate to the value of £7, carved at a cost of a further £20. The inscription was composed by Moray's friend, the scholar, George Buchanan.

The list below corresponds to the map which follows of places Moray would have known.

Key to Map

1.   Dunnottar Castle, Aberdeenshire
2.   Palace of Holyroodhouse, Edinburgh
3.   Palace of Westminster, London
4.   Perth
5.   Stirling Castle
6.   Inverness Castle
7.   Corrichie, Aberdeenshire
8.   Newcastle, England
9.   Jedburgh, Roxburghshire
10.   Lochleven Castle, Perthshire

11.   Langside, near Glasgow

12.   York, England

13.   Dumbarton Castle

14.   Linlithgow, near Edinburgh

15.   High Kirk of St Giles, Edinburgh

Map

Chapter 20: Three Book Reviews

There are no up-to-date biographies of Moray – as in life, he is largely relegated to a walk-on part in the lives of his sister, Mary, Queen of Scots, and his nephew, James VI. Three books which cover the period are: Robert Stedall's *'The Survival of the Crown'*, John Matusiak's *'James I'* and Rosalind Marshall's *'John Knox'*.

Three books we have reviewed that we recommend for an understanding of the period are detailed here.

The Challenge to the Crown (Vol I)

Author: Robert Stedall

Publisher: The Book Guild Ltd

In a nutshell A detailed analysis of the plots, and counterplots that characterised the reign of Mary, Queen of Scots, with credible insight into the complex motivations of those involved.

Mr Stedall did not begin his career as a professional historian, but that does not handicap his ability to pick his way through the complex politics at the court of Mary, Queen of Scots. He begins the narrative with a description of the situation in Scotland in the early 1540s – the King dead, the struggle for the Regency, and the looming threat of England. He then carries us into France with the little Queen, sent there for safety aged five. Stedall covers Mary's childhood and education in some detail. There is useful information about the politics of France, peppered with some of the more scandalous details of the French courts' love affairs, and background about Catherine de Medici.

He examines the political implications of the marriage of Mary to the Dauphin of Scotland, and that the ceding of the Crown Matrimonial to François meant that Mary's natural heir, the Duke of Chatelherault, and his son the Earl of Arran, were given a reason to join the Lords of the Congregation in their opposition to the Regency of Mary's mother. As Mary grew to adulthood in France, Scotland's elite, with the exception of her mother, the Queen-Regent, were turning away from the Auld Alliance with Catholic France, and seeking to join in common cause with Protestant England.

Stedwall gives an excellent summary of the position in Scotland and the alignment of the various factions on Mary's return as a widow from France. He makes it clear that combination in factions was not just a religious matter. The Catholic Huntly and the Protestant Bothwell were both opposed to the Protestant Moray, who was pro an alliance with England. Stedall, unlike many other writers, believes that Moray always entertained ambitions to snatch his half-sister's throne, but was willing to content himself with being her chief advisor, until the advent of her second husband, Lord Darnley.

In describing her reign, Stedall concludes that Mary, whilst clever and astute in many ways, and adept at gathering personal support *'showed political naivety and a misjudgement of people'*. He also convincingly demonstrates that her marriage to Darnley was a headstrong act, undertaken almost entirely without support from any of her nobles and saddled her with a fatal liability.

Stedall takes a different approach to the murder of Rizzio, from that espoused by John Guy in *'My Heart is My Own'*. It is Stedall's contention that Darnley intended Mary and their unborn child to die after the shock of witnessing the murder, with the goal of claiming the Crown himself, through his own Stewart blood (although the Duke of Chatelherault was widely accepted as the next heir.)

The narrative of Darnley's death is complex, as the subject itself is complex. Stedall's view is that Mary was innocent of the murder, and the whole plot was masterminded by Moray from start to finish, with Bothwell being manipulated into thinking it his own idea, and actually arranging it. Mary is shown as walking into the trap of appearing to be complicit in the murder of Darnley and her apparent abduction, by being too shamed by having slept with Bothwell (whether willingly or not) to refuse to marry him. Stedall concludes, however, that Mary's own failure to listen to sensible advice, and her stupidity in marrying Bothwell, despite it being evident that he had been involved in Darnley's murder, were the ultimate causes of her downfall.

This first volume in a two-volume work ends with Mary's deposition and Moray's acceptance as Regent.

Stendall's style is readable, and I received the impression that he knew the details of his subject well. Where the writer's inexperience perhaps shows is in a few places where the narrative becomes confused. Occasionally, lots of pronouns rather than names mean it is unclear exactly who was doing what to whom – the tendency of all the participants in the politics of the 1550s and 1560s to change sides and betray each other making it difficult to infer the identities from the context.

Annoyingly, the kindle version of the book has jumbled footnotes that merge into the text.

Crown of Thistles: the Fatal Inheritance of Mary, Queen of Scots
Author: Dr Linda Porter

Publisher: Macmillan

In a nutshell: An original take on a tale that has been told many times. Excellent both for readers new to the period and experts.

The sub-title of this book refers to the fatal inheritance of Mary, Queen of Scots, but this is actually a panoramic look at the relationship between the monarchs of England and Scotland between the 1480s and the Union of the Crowns in 1603 – although the period of Mary's incarceration in England and the 15 years after her death are dealt with more as a tidying up of loose ends.

Porter manages to convey a huge amount of information about all of the protagonists in very readable format. The depth of her research across the whole spectrum of people and events is impressive.

This extensive knowledge has allowed Porter to contest some of the frequently repeated judgements on many of the people and events involved. For example she is kinder to Margaret Tudor, the widow of James IV, than most historians have been – seeing Margaret as well-intentioned and determined to do the best for her son's realm. She also challenges the frequently repeated assertion that, post-Flodden, with a generation of leaders dead on the field, Scotland descended into chaos.

This is not, however, a dreary recitation of political facts. Porter covers a wide range of topics, from the architectural interests of Henry VIII, and the literary pursuits of James V, to the religious views of John Knox and the Machiavellian plotting of Mary's mother-in-law, Catherine de Medici.

Porter's Mary, too, is more nuanced than is often the case. She is shown as physically extremely courageous, charismatic, resourceful and politically shrewd in many ways, but Porter hints, although does not conclude, that Mary was probably aware of the plot to murder Darnley, even if she were not directly responsible.

Mary's actions after the death of Darnley seem to fly in the face of common sense, but hindsight is a marvellous thing, and it is difficult to unknow the results. At the time, Mary was surrounded by factions and traitors and each individual choice she made can be justified, although the outcome was disastrous. Her worst mistake of all was stepping into the fishing boat that took her across the Solway Firth and into twenty years of incarceration at the hands of her cousin, Elizabeth I.

The book is a weighty tome, but I wish it had been longer. An exposition by Porter of the years of plot and counterplot as Mary was pitted against Elizabeth's spymaster, Sir Francis Walsingham, would make gripping reading.

My Heart is My Own

Author: John Guy

Publisher: Harper Perennial UK

In a nutshell A compelling interpretation of Mary, Queen of Scots' character and motivations. Guy has put the central drama of Mary's life – the murder of Darnley – into its political context and gives a very credible theory as to the truth of events.

John Guy is an experienced and well-respected historian who has written on topics as diverse as Thomas Becket and Henry VIII's children. His academic credentials, however, have not damaged his ability to write a clear narrative of events – something that is very necessary in the extremely complex political world that surrounded Mary, Queen of Scots.

Mary has been a controversial figure from the time of her second marriage, and given her obvious intelligence and charisma, it has always been hard to understand how she could have acted in ways that, in retrospect, appear to be completely lacking in the most basic common sense, let alone political skill. By using, wherever possible, the contemporary letters and papers, Guy demonstrates that most (if not all) of Mary's actions were logical and understandable within the context of the information she had available. For what comes across very clearly, is that Mary did not always have the facts in her possession that would have enabled her to make different choices.

In so far as history books have villains, then William Cecil, Secretary of State to Queen Elizabeth I of England, is, in this book, a villain of the deepest hue. In Guy's interpretation, his constant interference in Scottish politics and his unshakeable enmity towards the Catholic Queen whom he saw as a threat to a Protestant succession in England destabilised an already unstable Scottish court. Guy is also very scathing of the part that Queen Mary's Guise relatives played. Her devotion to them, and her trust in their advice, are shown to be misplaced – they cared far more for their own aggrandisement in France than for their niece in faraway Scotland, although they never hesitated to use her for their own ends.

Guy is clearly sympathetic to Mary, but he cannot avoid the judgement that she threw her Crown away when she became entangled with Bothwell. His interpretation is that, although her abduction was forced, she was not raped, and that she married Bothwell willingly. This is a different interpretation from that of Porter, in 'Crown of Thistles' and a comparison of both books is valuable.

Guy's review of the investigation into the murder of Darnley, and the Casket Letters, is extremely detailed and gives a very welcome analysis of the actual evidence against the Queen – he also shows how and why it may have been fabricated.

Similarly, he gives a coherent and structured narrative of the various political imperatives that Mary was subjected to once she was imprisoned in England, and how, eventually, Mary had no choice but to support plots against Elizabeth, if she were to have any hope of regaining her freedom.

All in all, this is an excellent retelling of a well-known, but complex, story that has invited blind partisanship from many authors. Guy is clearly a supporter of Mary, and inevitably gives a positive interpretation of events where motivations are in question, but where Mary's actions were obviously wrong or foolish, he does not hesitate to say so.

Bibliography

Bingham, Caroline, *Darnley: A Life of Henry Stuart, Lord Darnley, Consort of Mary Queen of Scots* (London: Constable, 1995)

Blakeway, Amy, 'The Response to the Assassination of the Regent Moray', *Scottish Historical Review*, 88 (2009), 9–33 <http://dx.doi.org/10.3366/shr>

Calendar of Border Papers: Volume 1, 1560-95' <http://www.british-history.ac.uk/cal-border-papers/vol1/> [accessed 12 November 2015]

Calendar of State Papers: Scotland' <http://www.british-history.ac.uk/cal-state-papers/scotland> [accessed 10 November 2015]

Knox, John, *The Works of John Knox Vols 1 - 6*, ed. by David Laing (United Kingdom: James Thin, 1895)

Mackie, J D, *Calendar of the State Papers Relating to Scotland and Mary, Queen of Scots, 1547-1603: Preserved in the Public RecordOffice, the British Museum and Elsewhere* (Edinburgh: H.M.S.O (for the Scottish Record Office), 1969)

Marshall, Rosalind Kay K, *John Knox* (Edinburgh: Birlinn, 2008)

Melville, James Sir, Gordon Donaldson, and Melville, James Sir, *The Memoirs of Sir James Melville of Halhill, Containing an Impartial Account of the Most Remarkable Affairs of State during the Sixteenth Century Not Mentioned by Other Historians, More Particularly Relating to the Kingdoms of England and Scotland under* (London: Folio Society, 1969)

Rome: 1568, January-June' <http://www.british-history.ac.uk/cal-state-papers/vatican/vol1/pp268-281> [accessed 26 December 2015]

Stedall, Robert, *The Challenge to the Crown: The Struggle for Influence in the Reign of Mary, Queen of Scots 1542 - 1567*, 1st edn (Sussex, England: Book Guild Publishing, 2012)

Stedall, Robert, *The Survival of the Crown Volume II: The Return to Authority of the Scottish Crown Following Mary Queen of Scots' Deposition from the Throne 1567-1603*, Kindle (Book Guild Publishing, 2014)

Treasurer, Scotland, Scottish Record Office, and Thomas Dickson, *Accounts of the Lord High Treasurer of Scotland =: Compota Thesaurariorum Regum Scotorum* (Edinburgh: H.M. General Register House, 1877-, 1877)

Venice: *April 1566'* <http://www.british-history.ac.uk/cal-state-papers/venice/vol7/pp375-380> [accessed 26 December 2015]

www.tudortimes.co.uk

Printed in Great Britain
by Amazon

16465419R00048